Become a Better

L10

HOST

20 Proven Strategies To Improve Your Meetings Immediately!

Written by Paul King

TABLE OF CONTENTS

PREFACE

You will probably notice there are several recurring themes in the 20 lessons needed to improve your meetings. Things like:

- Respect others' time.
- Increase accountability.
- Improve productivity.
- Encourage quieter members.
- Enhance team cohesion.
- And celebrate wins.

How do you put these examples into your "real" meeting?

First a little background on myself:

I'm the Director of Sales and Marketing for a multi-seven figure business twice recognized on the Inc. 5000 as being one of the fastest growing in the nation.

In addition, I'm also the Integrator and Facilitator for the business, as well as a meeting consultant to businesses just like yours.

Previously I was the host of my own entertainment talk show on a 100,000 watt FM station that stretched from Tampa to Miami. Thankfully it became the #1 show on radio during my time slot for the demographic I was hoping to hit. I've interviewed everyone from celebrities and business leaders, to the local car salesman. In addition I've been on national TV, on stage in front of thousands of people, and currently host several podcasts.

There's <u>one thing</u> I've learned to be absolutely true in every sense - one thing that will *immediately* change how you think about hosting your meeting and how your meetings operate - but first, you'll need to learn these *essential* 20 lessons:

#1 The Structured Agenda

Let's dive into a conversational exploration on the importance of sticking to a structured agenda in meetings, illustrated through the journey of a real-world company we'll call "XYZ-ABC." This tale not only shines a light on the significance of disciplined meeting management but also gives us some insights into the transformative power of order and focus within a team setting.

The Prelude: Chaos in the Conference Room

Imagine XYZ-ABC Innovations, a bustling startup in the renewable energy sector, buzzing with ideas and innovation but hitting a snag when it came to execution. Picture their conference room: a roundtable of eager faces, each with brilliant ideas, but meetings that felt more like a ship adrift at sea—no compass, no map, no destination in sight. Discussions would start on one topic, meander through a dozen others, and circle back without landing. Sounds familiar, doesn't it? It was clear they needed a change.

The Revelation: Enter the Structured Agenda

During a particularly long and unproductive meeting, Alex, the COO, proposed an experiment: "What if we actually stick to our agenda next time? Like, really stick to it, no side tracks." There were skeptical looks around the table. But the team was desperate enough to try anything.

The Transformation Begins

The first meeting with a "strict adherence to agenda" rule felt a bit like putting on a new pair of shoes—uncomfortable at first, but promising. They outlined a clear agenda: a quick check-in, a review of ongoing projects, a deep dive into new proposals, followed by action items, all within a 60-minute window.

The Challenges and Triumphs

Challenge #1: The Tangent Temptation

Old habits die hard. When the team started to veer off course, Alex gently but firmly steered them back. "Let's park that idea for now and stay on track," became a familiar refrain.

Triumph #1: Discovering Efficiency

To everyone's surprise, the meeting ended on time, with every agenda item covered. It was a revelation. "We've never gotten through the whole agenda before!" someone exclaimed. The structured approach was working.

Challenge #2: FOMO on Flexibility

Some team members felt the structured agenda stifled creativity. "Where's the room for spontaneous ideas?"

they asked. The solution? Allocating a specific "wild card" segment in the agenda for open brainstorming, ensuring creativity had its time and place without derailing the meeting.

Triumph #2: Ideas with Impact

The "wild card" segment became one of the most productive parts of the meeting. Ideas were more focused, and because there was a designated time for creative brainstorming, the team felt more present during the structured segments.

The Ripple Effect

The changes in the conference room began to ripple through the entire organization. Project teams adopted the structured agenda approach, leading to more efficient meetings across the board. It wasn't just about sticking to the agenda; it was about respect—respect for each other's time, ideas, and the collective mission of XYZ-ABC Innovations.

The Evolution: A Culture of Productivity

Six months into this experiment, XYZ-ABC's meetings had transformed. What started as an exercise in discipline had evolved into a culture of productivity and respect. Meetings became something the team looked forward to, not because they were a break from work, but because they were an integral part of their success.

The Testimonial

Reflecting on the journey, Alex shared, "I never realized how much time we wasted until we stopped wasting it. Following a strict agenda didn't just make our meetings more efficient; it made us a more focused, more cohesive team. It's like we found our compass and map, and now we're all rowing in the same direction."

The Takeaway

XYZ-ABC Innovations' story is a testament to the power of structure within creativity, discipline within freedom. It shows that a strict adherence to a structured agenda isn't about stifling discussion but about ensuring that every voice is heard, every idea is considered, and every meeting moves the needle forward.

So, next time you find yourself in a meeting that's going off the rails, remember XYZ-ABC's journey. A little structure can go a long way in turning chaos into clarity, ideas into action, and meetings into milestones on the road to success.

#2 Starting and Ending Meetings On Time

Let's talk about something that might sound deceptively simple but is actually a game-changer in the business world: starting and ending meetings on time. Now, I know what you might be thinking, "Surely, that can't be that big of a deal, right?" But let me walk you through a real-life story that highlights just how impactful this practice can be. This is the story of a company we'll call "XYZ-DEF," a creative agency that learned the hard way the importance of punctuality in meetings.

The Pre-Change Scenario at XYZ-DEF

XYZ-DEF was your typical bustling creative agency, filled with passionate employees who thrived on innovation and creativity. However, there was one problem that seemed to be the bane of their existence: meetings. Meetings at XYZ-DEF were notorious for starting late and running over time. It became such an issue that it was almost a company joke, but the consequences were far from funny.

Projects were falling behind schedule, team members were frustrated, and there was a palpable tension in the air. The leadership team, while excellent in their creative endeavors, struggled with time management. This lack of punctuality not only affected the efficiency of their meetings but also began to seep into the company's culture, affecting overall morale and productivity.

The Turning Point

The turning point came when a key client threatened to take their business elsewhere due to repeated delays in project delivery. This was a wake-up call for the leadership team. They realized they needed to make a change, and fast. After some reflection and consultation, they decided to focus on one seemingly small but significant change: ensuring that all meetings started and ended on time.

Implementing the Change

The first step in implementing this change was to set clear expectations. The leadership team communicated to everyone that punctuality would be a priority. They introduced new guidelines for meetings, including setting clear agendas ahead of time, establishing firm start and end times, and implementing a policy where meetings would proceed regardless of whether everyone was present.

At first, there was some skepticism. "Can a few minutes here and there really make that much of a difference?" was a common sentiment. However, as the new policy was put into practice, the benefits became increasingly apparent.

The Impact of Timely Meetings

<u>Respect for Everyone's Time</u>: One of the immediate effects of this new policy was an increased respect for

everyone's time. Team members began to appreciate the predictability of meetings starting and ending as planned, which allowed them to manage their own schedules more effectively.

Increased Meeting Efficiency: With strict time limits in place, meetings became more focused and efficient. The agendas were adhered to more closely, and as a result, decisions were made faster, and fewer meetings were needed to achieve the same outcomes (the dreaded, "we'll put it off until next week").

Improved Morale: This newfound efficiency led to a noticeable improvement in team morale. Employees felt their time was valued, which increased their engagement and satisfaction at work. The culture of the company began to shift from one of frustration and tardiness to one of professionalism and respect.

Better Client Relationships: As internal meetings became more efficient, this punctuality and professionalism were reflected in client meetings as well. XYZ-DEF was able to rebuild trust with their clients, demonstrating that they respected their time and were committed to meeting deadlines.

Boosted Creativity and Innovation: Interestingly, by having more structured and punctual meetings, team members found they had more time for creative thinking and innovation. The discipline imposed by the meeting schedules freed up mental space and time for creativity to flourish.

Reflections from XYZ-DEF

A year into this change, the leadership team at XYZ-DEF reflected on the impact. It was clear that something as simple as starting and ending meetings on time had a profound effect on the company's operations, culture, and bottom line. Projects were back on track, client relationships were stronger than ever, and the team felt more cohesive and motivated.

In a candid conversation, the CEO of XYZ-DEF shared, "We never realized how much of an impact punctuality could have. It was a small change that led to big results. Our meetings are now something we look forward to because we know they'll be productive and that we're respecting each other's time."

Conclusion

The story of XYZ-DEF serves as a powerful reminder of the importance of punctuality in meetings. It's not just about being professional; it's about creating a culture of respect, efficiency, and productivity. So next time you're scheduling a meeting, remember XYZ-DEF's story. A timely start and end might just be the simplest yet most effective change you can make to drive your team forward.

#3 Preparation is Key

Creating a culture where preparation is paramount for meetings can transform the way a company operates, sparking efficiency, engagement, and clarity across all levels. Let's dive into a case study of XYZ-GHI, a tech startup that went from chaotic brainstorming sessions to streamlined, productive meetings by championing one principle: Preparation is key.

The Before Picture

Imagine a startup, buzzing with ideas, energy, and potential. That was XYZ-GHI in its early days. Weekly team meetings were meant to be the engine room of innovation. Yet, more often than not, they turned into directionless chats. Why? Because "winging it" had become the norm. Team members would show up, sometimes late, with a vague idea of what they wanted to discuss, leading to meandering conversations that rarely concluded with actionable decisions.

The Turning Point

Enter Clara, XYZ-GHI's newly appointed COO. Clara observed the chaos and saw an opportunity. She introduced a simple yet revolutionary idea: "What if everyone came prepared?" At first, this question was met with mixed reactions. Some saw it as common sense they'd simply been overlooking, while others were skeptical, questioning how much difference preparation could truly make.

Implementing the Change

Clara didn't just demand change; she facilitated it. She started with clear guidelines on what being prepared meant:

- Agenda Items: Everyone was to contribute to the meeting agenda at least 24 hours in advance.

- Pre-Reads: Relevant documents or updates were to be shared alongside the agenda, giving everyone a chance to come informed.

- Defined Objectives: Each agenda item needed a goal. Was it a decision, an update, or a brainstorming session?

The First Few Meetings

The initial shift was, to put it mildly, a bit rocky. Old habits die hard. The first meeting under the new regime had its share of blank stares and incomplete updates. But Clara remained patient, emphasizing the long-term gains over short-term discomfort.

The Breakthrough

About a month in, things began to change. Meetings started to feel different. Here's what happened:

- <u>Efficiency Skyrocketed</u>: With everyone coming in prepared, meetings that used to drag on for hours were now wrapping up in half the time. This wasn't just about speed; it was about focus. Discussions were sharper, more on-point.

- <u>Engagement Increased</u>: Preparation led to confidence. Team members who used to stay silent, unsure of how to contribute, were now joining the conversation. They had insights to share, backed by the pre-reads and their own prep.

- <u>Better Decision-Making</u>: With all the relevant information on the table from the get-go, decisions were made faster and with a clearer understanding of their implications.

A Culture Shift

XYZ-GHI's meeting culture underwent a transformation. Preparation became a sign of professionalism and respect for each other's time. It fostered a deeper sense of accountability and ownership over the meeting's outcomes.

A Ripple Effect

The impact of this shift went beyond just meetings. It permeated the company's culture, affecting how projects were managed and how teams collaborated. XYZ-GHI started seeing:

- <u>Improved Project Timelines</u>: With clearer decisions and actionable takeaways from meetings, projects moved forward more predictably and efficiently.

- <u>Increased Innovation</u>: With the foundation of each meeting solidified by preparation, the team could afford to spend time on creative brainstorming, knowing they had a structured way to evaluate and follow up on ideas.

Looking Back and Forward

Clara and her team at XYZ-GHI learned a valuable lesson: Preparation doesn't stifle spontaneity; it channels it. By coming prepared, they didn't just make their meetings more efficient; they made them more meaningful.

Conversational Nuggets

In a chat with Clara about the journey, she shared some nuggets of wisdom:

- "Preparation is contagious." Once a few team members saw the benefits, the rest followed.

- "It's about respect." Coming prepared shows respect for your colleagues' time and contributions.

- "Preparation breeds confidence." Team members who feel prepared are more likely to speak up and share their ideas.

Final Thoughts

XYZ-GHI's story is a testament to the power of preparation in transforming meetings from time-drains into engines of productivity and innovation. It shows that with the right approach and a commitment to change, meetings can be more than just a calendar obligation—they can be a catalyst for growth and success.

#4 Setting Clear Objectives

In the bustling world of corporate dynamics, where time is as precious as insights, the saga of XYZ-JKL serves as a beacon for the transformative power of clear meeting objectives. Let's unpack their story in a conversational stroll through the corridors of change, highlighting the essence of focused and productive discussions.

The Prequel: A Common Scenario

XYZ-JKL, much like any ambitious enterprise, thrived on innovation and collaboration. Yet, their meetings had become infamous for being black holes of time and energy. Picture this: a room full of bright minds, each buzzing with ideas, yet conversations zigzagging without a clear destination. It was a classic case of motion without progress, leaving participants more perplexed than empowered.

Catalyst for Change: The Epiphany

The turning point came unexpectedly during one particularly aimless meeting when Mia, a project manager with a knack for keen observations, noted the palpable frustration. She mused aloud, "What if we're missing the map because we haven't decided where we want to go?" That simple question struck a chord. The issue wasn't the lack or quality of ideas; it was the absence of clear objectives guiding each meeting.

The Strategy: Setting Clear Objectives

Emboldened by this revelation, the leadership team, with Mia taking the lead, embarked on a mission to redefine their meeting culture. The strategy was straightforward yet profound: every meeting would start with a clear statement of its objectives.

Implementation: The First Steps

The new approach was simple in theory but required a shift in mindset. Here's how XYZ-JKL began the transformation:

- <u>Objective-Driven Agendas</u>: Each meeting agenda began with a clear objective, answering the "why" of the meeting. It wasn't just about discussing project updates; it was about defining what success in those discussions looked like.

- <u>Pre-Meeting Briefs</u>: To ensure everyone was on the same page, pre-meeting briefs circulated, outlining the objectives and providing context. This ensured that the meeting time was spent diving into discussions with a shared understanding of the goals.

The Impact: A Ripple of Productivity

The change didn't happen overnight, but the effects started to show. Meetings became more than a routine;

they transformed into strategic touchpoints that propelled projects forward.

- Focused Discussions: With clear objectives in place, discussions became more focused. The wandering conversations of the past gave way to targeted dialogues that drove action.

- Efficient Use of Time: Meetings began and ended on time, respecting everyone's schedule. The efficiency wasn't just in adherence to time but in the value extracted from each minute spent in the meeting room.

- Empowered Participation: Knowing the objectives ahead of time empowered team members to prepare and contribute more meaningfully. This inclusivity enriched the meetings with diverse perspectives, directly tied to the objectives at hand.

The Cultural Shift: From Meetings to Milestones

What XYZ-JKL experienced was not just an improvement in meetings but a cultural shift. Meetings became milestones in the journey of projects, markers of progress, and platforms for decisive action.

Conversational Insights: The Heart of Change

In a candid conversation with Mia, she reflected on the journey:

- "It was about giving direction to our energy." Clear objectives acted as a compass, guiding the collective energy towards a common goal.

- "Meetings became moments of clarity." The clarity in objectives turned meetings into opportunities for alignment and clear next steps.

- "We learned the art of concise conversations." With objectives guiding the way, conversations became more purposeful, shedding the excess and focusing on essence.

XYZ-JKL's Echo: A Testament to Transformation

XYZ-JKL's story is a testament to the power of clarity in driving productivity and focus in meetings. It's a narrative that echoes in the halls of many organizations, a reminder that the first step towards meaningful discussions is setting clear objectives.

The Takeaway: A Universal Lesson

The lesson from XYZ-JKL is universal. Whether you're a startup on the brink of discovery or an established enterprise navigating through growth, the clarity of meeting objectives is the keystone of productive discussions. It's a principle that transcends industries, a simple yet profound truth: clarity leads to focus, and focus leads to progress.

Final Thoughts: A Conversation Starter

As we wrap up this conversational journey through XYZ-JKL's transformation, let's take it as a conversation starter. Think about the last meeting you attended. Did it have a clear objective? Imagine the potential of every meeting being a focused, productive dialogue, each a step forward in the collective journey of your team or organization.

XYZ-JKL's story is more than a case study; it's a blueprint for elevating the quality of our collaborations, one meeting at a time. Let's take that step, guided by clear objectives, towards a future where every meeting is a milestone.

#5 Limiting Tangential Conversations

In the bustling world of modern business, where every minute counts, there's a subtle art to keeping meetings on track. This art became vividly clear through the journey of a dynamic startup named XYZ-MNO. Their story is a quintessential example of how limiting tangential conversations can transform meeting culture, ensuring focus and productivity. So, grab a cup of coffee, and let's delve into their enlightening experience.

The Scene at XYZ-MNO

XYZ-MNO, born out of a garage, had the energy, the ideas, and the momentum. As they grew, so did their meetings—both in frequency and length. Initially, these gatherings felt like brainstorming goldmines. However, as time went on, the goldmines started turning into time-consuming detours. Meetings became arenas for endless tangents, with the team often finding themselves discussing everything but the agenda.

The Moment of Realization

It was during a routine quarterly review that Alex, the CEO, noted a concerning pattern: despite lengthy meetings, key projects were lagging. The management team gathered for what was supposed to be a strategic session, only to find themselves sidetracked by a debate over the new office coffee blend. It was a lightbulb moment for Alex. The issue wasn't a lack of dedication or ideas; it was the unchecked drift into tangential conversations.

The Strategy Shift

Determined to steer meetings back on course, Alex introduced a simple yet powerful strategy: "The Tangent Bin." This was a literal bin (initially a notepad, later a digital document) where off-topic ideas and discussions could be "tossed" to be revisited later, ensuring they weren't lost but didn't derail the meeting's focus.

Implementing the Change

The first few attempts were rocky. Again, old habits die hard, and the team initially struggled to differentiate between productive digressions and tangential drifts. However, Alex remained patient, guiding the team with gentle reminders and the visual cue of the Tangent Bin sitting prominently in every meeting.

The Transformation

Over time, a fascinating transformation occurred within XYZ-MNO's meeting rooms:

- <u>Meetings Became Shorter and More Productive</u>: With the Tangent Bin in place, discussions remained focused on the agenda. Projects that were previously stalled due to indecision or lack of clarity were now moving forward with renewed vigor.

- <u>The Team Became More Engaged</u>: Knowing that their off-topic ideas wouldn't be dismissed but rather saved for a *relevant time*, team members felt more valued and listened to. This led to an increase in engagement and participation.

- <u>Innovation Didn't Suffer</u>; It Flourished: A significant concern was that curtailing tangential conversations would stifle creativity. The opposite proved true. With more focused discussions, when it came time to open the Tangent Bin in designated brainstorming sessions, the ideas were richer and more diverse.

- <u>Respect for Time Cultivated Respect for Ideas</u>: As meetings became more disciplined, the team started valuing the time and contributions of their peers more deeply. This cultivated an environment of respect and collaboration that extended beyond the meeting room.

Key Lessons and Conversational Insights

Reflecting on the journey, Alex shared some key insights in a candid chat:

- "It's about balance, not suppression": The goal was never to stifle conversation but to channel it constructively. The Tangent Bin allowed them to maintain this balance.

- "Visibility matters": Having a physical (or virtual) bin made the concept tangible, serving as a constant reminder of the meeting's objectives.

- "Flexibility is key": Not all tangents are bad. Sometimes, what seems off-topic at first glance could lead to valuable insights. *The trick lies in discerning which is which and being flexible enough to adjust on the fly.*

- "Engagement doesn't mean agreement": Encouraging focused discussions also meant fostering an environment where dissenting opinions could be voiced and considered without fear of derailing the conversation.

The Ripple Effect

The success of this strategy extended beyond just meeting efficiency. XYZ-MNO saw a marked improvement in project timelines, team morale, and overall company culture. Meetings transformed from dreaded calendar entries to productive, engaging sessions where real progress was made.

Wrapping Up with a Bow

XYZ-MNO's journey from chaos to clarity is a compelling testament to the power of limiting tangential conversations. It underscores a universal truth in business: time is the most precious commodity. By safeguarding it within meetings, we can unlock the full potential of our teams and projects.

As we close this chapter on XYZ-MNO, let's carry forward the lesson that sometimes, the most impactful changes stem from the simplest of shifts in perspective and practice. So, the next time you find yourself in a meeting veering off course, remember the tale of XYZ-MNO and consider whether it's time to introduce a Tangent Bin of your own.

#6 Foster Active Participation

Let's dive into the transformative journey of a company called XYZ-STU, a medium-sized graphic design firm that faced a common yet critical challenge: making their meetings more than just a routine gathering. The story of how they embraced the principle of "Active Participation" to rejuvenate their meetings and decision-making process is not just instructional but downright inspiring. So, grab your favorite beverage, and let's get into the details.

The Starting Point

XYZ-STU had its fair share of successes, but there was a hitch in their stride. Their meetings had become somewhat of a monologue, dominated by a few voices, while the rest of the team remained passive spectators. Ideas and decisions were getting through, but something crucial was missing: the collective intelligence of the team.

The Revelation

Enter Maya, a newly appointed team lead with fresh eyes and a keen sense of observation. She noticed the untapped potential sitting silently around the meeting table. Maya believed that every team member, regardless of their title, had valuable insights that could propel the company forward. The challenge was to shift the meeting culture from passive to active participation.

The Strategy

Maya knew that change wouldn't happen overnight, but she was determined. She introduced a few ground rules aimed at fostering an environment where everyone felt compelled and comfortable to contribute:

- <u>Equal Floor Time</u>: Implementing a round-robin approach to ensure that everyone had the chance to speak.

- <u>No Idea is Too Small</u>: Encouraging the team to share any and all ideas, fostering an environment where creativity knows no bounds.

- <u>Question Everything</u>: Promoting a culture of curiosity where questioning and digging deeper into ideas was not just allowed but expected.

The Implementation

The first few meetings under the new regime were awkward. People were unaccustomed to being asked for their input so directly. However, Maya was patient, often prompting quieter team members for their thoughts and publicly celebrating all contributions, regardless of the outcome.

The Turning Point

A few weeks in, something remarkable happened. During a brainstorming session for a major project, a junior designer, Alex, hesitantly suggested an unconventional idea. Initially, the room went silent, but Maya seized the moment to explore the idea further. This led to a lively discussion, and ultimately, Alex's concept became the foundation of one of the most successful campaigns XYZ-STU had ever launched.

The Impact

This moment was a catalyst for change at XYZ-STU. Meetings transformed from mundane to meaningful, as everyone started to come prepared, eager to contribute. The impact of active participation was profound:

- Enhanced Creativity: With diverse perspectives on the table, the team started to think outside the box, leading to innovative solutions and ideas.

- Improved Decision Making: Decisions were no longer one-sided. They were enriched with the collective input of the team, leading to more robust and well-rounded outcomes.

- Increased Engagement: Meetings became something the team looked forward to. They knew their voice mattered, which boosted morale and job satisfaction.

The Ripple Effect

The benefits of active participation didn't stop at meetings. It spilled over into the company culture, fostering a sense of belonging and ownership among team members. People were more engaged, not just with their work but with each other, leading to a more cohesive and collaborative team dynamic.

The Conversation

In a candid conversation, Maya shared some insights into the journey:

- "It's about empowerment." Making sure everyone knows their input is valued makes them feel empowered and integral to the team's success.

- "Active participation is a skill." Like any skill, it takes practice and encouragement to develop. It's important to create a safe space for people to express themselves.

- "Diversity of thought is our greatest asset." Leveraging the varied perspectives of the team leads to better outcomes and a more inclusive work environment.

Final Thoughts

The story of XYZ-STU is a powerful reminder of the untapped potential within teams. By fostering a culture of active participation, they not only improved their meetings and decision-making process but also transformed their work environment into one where everyone feels valued and engaged. This approach to meetings can serve as a blueprint for any organization looking to harness the collective intelligence of their team, proving that when everyone contributes, the possibilities are limitless.

#7 Effective Time Management

Let's dive into a real-life scenario at XYZ-VWX, a bustling tech startup that found itself at a critical juncture. The team, brimming with talent and ideas, was struggling to keep pace with its ambitious roadmap. The culprit? Meetings that seemed to stretch on indefinitely without covering all the necessary ground. The solution that transformed their trajectory was rooted in one principle: effective time management within meetings.

The Prelude: Where Time Slipped Away

XYZ-VWX was your typical high-energy startup. Ideas flowed as freely as the coffee, but so did the meetings. The leadership team noticed that while enthusiasm was high, productivity was taking a hit. Meetings were frequent and long, yet key decisions and action items were often deferred to follow-up meetings that suffered the same fate.

Aha Moment: The Need for Time Management

It was during one particularly lengthy strategy session, which veered off into an unplanned debate about office snacks, that the leadership had their aha moment. They realized that without structured time management, their meetings would continue to be inefficient and unproductive. That's when they decided to implement strict time limits for each agenda item.

Implementing Time Management: A Step-by-Step Change

The transformation didn't happen overnight. XYZ-VWX took a systematic approach to embed effective time management into their meeting culture:

1. <u>Agenda Preparation</u>: Every meeting now required a detailed agenda circulated in advance, with clear objectives and time allocations for each item.

2. <u>Timekeeper Role</u>: They introduced the role of a timekeeper for meetings, responsible for ensuring that discussions stayed within their allocated time slots.

3. <u>The "Parking Lot" Method</u>: Any topic that wasn't on the agenda or that threatened to overrun its time slot was placed in a "parking lot" to be addressed later, either in a designated follow-up or via email.

Early Challenges and Solutions

The initial response to these changes was mixed. Some team members chafed at what they saw as restrictions on creativity and discussion. However, the leadership team *led by example*, showing how disciplined time management actually freed up more time for deep, focused work on critical issues.

The Results: A Transformative Impact

Over the next few months, the impact of these changes became undeniable:

- <u>Meetings Became More Productive</u>: With clear time limits, discussions were more focused, decisions were made faster, and meetings ended with concrete action items.

- <u>Increased Accountability</u>: The discipline of adhering to time limits fostered a culture of accountability. Team members came to meetings better prepared, knowing they had a limited window to present their points.

- <u>Enhanced Morale</u>: As meetings became more efficient, team members felt their time was being respected. This led to improved morale and a more positive outlook on meetings as valuable rather than time-consuming.

- <u>Freed Up Time for Innovation</u>: By reducing the duration of meetings, Cascade Innovations found they had more time available for the creative and deep work that drove their success.

Conversational Insights from the Team

When talking to the team about the changes, a few key insights emerged:

- <u>Respect for Time is Respect for People</u>: Team members appreciated that the new approach showed respect for their time and contributions, making them more eager to participate.

- <u>Preparation is Paramount</u>: Knowing there were strict time limits encouraged better preparation, which in turn made the discussions more meaningful and productive.

- <u>Flexibility Within Structure</u>: While the time limits were strict, the team learned to be flexible within that structure, adapting as needed to ensure critical issues received the attention they deserved.

Reflecting on the Journey

Looking back, the leadership team at XYZ-VWX recognized that implementing effective time management in their meetings was a pivotal moment. It wasn't just about making meetings shorter; it was about *making every minute count*. This shift not only improved their meetings but also had a ripple effect on the company's culture, productivity, and ultimately, its success.

The Takeaway

XYZ-VWX' journey from time-drained to time-efficient meetings underscores a crucial lesson for all: Effective time management in meetings isn't about curtailing dialogue; it's about ensuring that every discussion, decision, and action item is given the space it needs within the bounds of respect for everyone's time. This approach can transform meetings from time sinks into catalysts for progress and innovation.

#8 Use a Timer

Let's chat about a little game-changer called "the timer" and how it revolutionized meetings at a bustling digital marketing firm, XYZ-YZ. Picture this: XYZ-YZ is thriving, teams are bustling with ideas, and the energy is palpable. But there's a hiccup—their meetings are a wild ride of epic proportions, sprawling discussions with no end in sight. Sounds familiar? Well, let's dive into how they tackled this with something as simple as a timer, making meetings not just bearable but incredibly effective.

The Before Times

XYZ-YZ's meetings were like marathons without a finish line. Ideas flew fast and furious, which sounds great on paper, but in reality? Decisions were rare, agendas were more like vague suggestions, and "end of meeting" was a myth. The team's enthusiasm was there, but focus? Not so much. This is where our hero, the timer, comes into play.

The Eureka Moment

Enter Alex, the newly minted team lead, fresh from a productivity workshop and armed with a novel idea: using a visible timer in meetings. The concept was disarmingly simple. Each agenda item gets a specific time allocation, and the timer keeps everyone honest. Skepticism was the initial response. "A timer? Are we baking a cake?" the team joked. But Alex was onto something.

Rolling Out the Timer

The first meeting with the timer felt a bit like a reality TV challenge. There it was, projected on the screen for all to see, ticking down. The agenda was divided into segments—project updates, brainstorming, action items—with clear time limits. The team embarked on this experiment with a mix of curiosity and apprehension.

The Immediate Impact

Something clicked. The ticking clock was a constant, gentle reminder: time is ticking, let's stay on track. Discussions were more focused, questions more pointed. The usual culprits of tangential debates were reined in, not by force, but by the collective understanding that time was of the essence.

Surprising Benefits

1. <u>Enhanced Focus</u>: Knowing there's only so much time to speak made everyone more prepared and concise in their contributions.

2. <u>Equal Participation</u>: The timer democratized meetings. With time limits, everyone had a chance to contribute, making meetings richer with diverse perspectives.

3. <u>Decisions Happened</u>: With less time wasted on digressions, decisions were made within the meeting, not deferred endlessly.

4. <u>Meetings Ended on Time</u>: Perhaps the most celebrated outcome. Meetings that used to meander past the hour now wrapped up with minutes to spare.

The Ripple Effect

The timer didn't just change how meetings were conducted; it sparked a broader cultural shift within XYZ-YZ. The value of time and the importance of preparation became ingrained in the team's ethos. The discipline fostered in meetings spilled over into how projects were managed and deadlines were met. The team started to respect each other's time more, not just in meetings but in all aspects of their work.

The Naysayers and the Converts

Of course, change is never without its challengers. Some team members felt the pressure of the clock stifled creativity. "Some ideas need time to breathe," they argued. Alex listened, adapting the approach. For brainstorming sessions where creativity needed to flow more freely, the timer was paused, ensuring a balance between structure and spontaneity.

The Long-Term Impact

Months down the line, the timer became an unspoken member of the team. Meetings that were once dreaded became productive power hours. The team learned to respect the timer, not as a taskmaster, but as a tool that amplified their efficiency and creativity.

Conversational Insights from the Team

- "I was skeptical about the timer, but now? I can't imagine meetings without it. It's like we found the secret sauce for productivity," said one team member.

- "The timer taught us the value of being concise. It's a skill, really, turning your thoughts into something coherent and quick," mused another.

- "It's not just about saving time; it's about respecting each other's time. That was the real lesson for us," reflected Alex.

Wrapping Up

XYZ-YZ's journey from time-bound chaos to streamlined efficiency is a testament to the power of simple solutions to complex problems. The timer, a modest tool, transformed how the team viewed and used their time, making every minute count. It's a story that proves sometimes, the smallest changes can bring about the most significant impacts, turning meetings from time sinks into treasure troves of productivity and innovation.

#9 Regular Review of To-Dos

In the bustling world of FinTech startups, where the pace is relentless and the stakes are high, the story of ABC-XYZ serves as a compelling case study on the transformative power of regular review of to-dos in meetings. This narrative isn't just about checking off boxes; it's about cultivating a culture of accountability, clarity, and shared purpose. So, grab a cup of coffee, and let's dive into Zenith's journey from chaos to clarity.

The Backstory

ABC-XYZ, a rising star in the FinTech sector, had its fair share of growing pains. Rapid expansion and the exhilarating rush of innovation were shadowed by a lingering issue: a lack of follow-through on action items. Meetings were energetic brainstorming sessions, but too often, ideas and tasks discussed one week seemed to vanish into thin air by the next.

The Aha Moment

The turning point came during a quarterly review when the leadership team, led by CEO Alex, noticed a recurring theme: many initiatives that were critical to their strategic goals hadn't moved an inch. Alex, reflecting on this pattern, realized the crux of the problem wasn't a lack of ideas or motivation but a failure in tracking and accountability. "We need a system," Alex mused, "a way to keep our to-dos front and center."

Implementing the Change

The solution was elegant in its simplicity: begin every meeting with a review of the to-dos from the previous meeting. This wasn't a groundbreaking idea, but its implementation was revolutionary for ABC-XYZ. Alex introduced this practice in the next all-hands meeting, emphasizing the importance of accountability and the role of this simple check-in in achieving their collective goals.

The First Few Meetings

The initial reactions were mixed. Some team members were skeptical, viewing this new practice as potentially micromanaging. However, as the weeks went by, the benefits became undeniable:

- <u>Clarity</u>: Starting meetings with a review of to-dos cut through the fog of day-to-day tasks, refocusing the team on what had been agreed upon as important.

- <u>Accountability</u>: Knowing there would be a check-in at the next meeting created a gentle but firm pressure to follow through on commitments.

- <u>Encouragement</u>: Celebrating completed tasks had an unexpectedly positive effect on morale. It wasn't just about holding people accountable; it was about recognizing their efforts and achievements.

The Transformation

Over the months, this simple practice reshaped ABC-XYZ's meeting culture and, by extension, their work culture. Meetings became more than just a space for discussion; they were a platform for accountability and progress.

- <u>Improved Project Completion Rates</u>: The regular review of to-dos led to a noticeable increase in the completion of action items, directly impacting project timelines and success rates.

- <u>Enhanced Team Cohesion</u>: This practice fostered a sense of shared responsibility and trust among team members. Everyone knew what others were working on and could offer help or resources to ensure those tasks were completed.

- <u>Increased Transparency</u>: The process demystified the status of various initiatives, making it clear where the team stood on its journey toward its goals.

The Ripple Effect

The impact of this practice reached beyond just improving meeting efficiency. It started affecting how team members approached their work and collaboration:

- <u>Proactive Problem-Solving</u>: Team members began to anticipate potential roadblocks to their to-dos and sought assistance or resources ahead of time.

- <u>Cross-Functional Collaboration</u>: As the status of tasks became more transparent, team members from different departments were more likely to offer help or collaborate, breaking down silos.

- <u>Strategic Alignment</u>: Regularly revisiting to-dos ensured that the team's daily efforts were aligned with the broader strategic goals of the company.

Reflections from the Team

In a candid conversation about the changes, a project manager shared, "It's about respect, really. Knowing that we'll review our to-dos makes me more mindful of what I commit to and more determined to deliver on it." Another team member added, "It's satisfying to share what you've accomplished and see how it fits into the bigger picture."

The Bottom Line

ABC-XYZ's journey from the chaotic enthusiasm of a burgeoning startup to a more structured, accountable organization underscores the power of regular review of to-dos in meetings. This practice isn't just about keeping track of tasks; it's about building a culture of accountability, transparency, and shared success. It's a reminder that sometimes, the simplest changes can lead to the most profound transformations.

#10 Focus on IDS

In the bustling world of business, meetings can often feel like a necessary evil—a time-consuming obligation that many dread, yet everyone recognizes as essential for progress. But what if I told you about a transformative approach that turned meetings from dreaded time sinks into engines of problem-solving and innovation? This is the story of ABC-DEF, a mid-sized tech company that revolutionized its meeting culture by embracing the "Identify, Discuss, Solve"™ (IDS) methodology, a cornerstone of the Entrepreneurial Operating System® (EOS).

The Pre-IDS Era at ABC-DEF

ABC-DEF was much like any other company, struggling with meetings that often felt aimless and unproductive. Their meetings were characterized by endless discussions, circular debates, and a palpable sense of frustration. Key issues lingered unresolved, leading to inefficiencies and stifled growth.

Discovery of IDS

The turning point came when Eli, a newly appointed operations manager with a keen interest in organizational efficiency, stumbled upon the IDS framework. Intrigued by its simplicity and potential for impact, Eli proposed to pilot the IDS approach in their weekly team meetings.

Implementing IDS

IDS stands for Identify, Discuss, Solve. It's a structured process that focuses meeting time on pinpointing key issues, engaging in targeted discussion, and developing actionable solutions. Eli introduced this concept to the team, emphasizing the importance of spending the majority of their meeting time on this process.

The First Steps

Initially, the team was skeptical. Change is often met with resistance, and this was no exception. However, Eli was persistent. He started each meeting by clearly stating the objective: "Today, we're here to tackle our biggest challenges head-on using the IDS process."

Identifying Key Issues

The first step, Identify, was about getting to the heart of the matter. Team members were encouraged to bring up any obstacles they faced, no matter how big or small. This phase was eye-opening. It turned out that many team members were struggling with issues others were either unaware of or assumed were already being addressed.

Discussing with Purpose

With the issues laid out, the team moved to the Discuss phase. This wasn't about rehashing old debates; it was focused, purposeful dialogue aimed at understanding the root causes. Eli *guided these discussions with a firm hand,* ensuring they remained on track and productive.

Solving as a Team

The Solve phase was where the magic happened. Solutions were proposed, debated briefly, and then decided upon. What made this different from previous attempts at problem-solving was the commitment to actionable solutions. If an idea was chosen, it was immediately assigned a "champion" and a deadline.

The Results

The impact of the IDS process on ABC-DEF was profound:

- <u>Meetings Became More Productive</u>: The team could cover more ground in less time because discussions were focused and driven by a clear objective.

- <u>Improved Problem-Solving</u>: The structured approach led to more effective solutions, as the team spent less time on irrelevant details and more time on addressing the core issues.

- <u>Increased Accountability</u>: By assigning champions and deadlines in the Solve phase, action items were tracked and followed through, leading to tangible improvements.

- <u>Enhanced Team Dynamics</u>: The IDS process democratized meetings. Everyone had a voice, and all perspectives were considered, leading to a stronger, more cohesive team.

A Cultural Shift

What started as an experiment in efficiency became a cornerstone of ABC-DEF' corporate culture. Meetings were no longer dreaded; they were anticipated as opportunities to make meaningful progress. The success of the IDS approach even caught the attention of other departments, leading to a company-wide adoption.

Reflections from Eli

In a candid conversation about the transformation, Eli shared, "Adopting IDS was about more than just making our meetings more efficient. It was about changing how we think about problems and solutions. It's a mindset that values action, accountability, and the collective intelligence of the team."

The Takeaway

ABC-DEF's journey from unproductive meetings to a problem-solving powerhouse is a testament to the power of structured processes like IDS. It shows that with the right approach, meetings can be more than just a necessary evil; they can be a catalyst for change, growth, and innovation.

The story of ABC-DEF serves as a compelling case for any organization looking to revamp its meeting culture. It's a reminder that the key to effective meetings lies not in avoiding them but in transforming them into focused, productive, and engaging sessions that drive results.

#11 Encourage Open and Honest Communication

In the bustling world of modern business, where every minute counts and every decision can pivot a company's direction, the value of open and honest communication in meetings cannot be overstated. Let's take a closer look at how one company, XYZ-MNO, transformed its culture and outcomes by prioritizing this principle.

The Backstory

XYZ-MNO, a once small startup that had grown into a significant player in the tech industry, was facing a crisis. Despite their growth, they found innovation stalling and employee morale waning. Meetings had become perfunctory, with the same voices dominating conversations and a palpable tension that left little room for genuine dialogue. Important issues were often skirted around, and feedback was either sugar-coated or not shared at all, leading to repeated mistakes and missed opportunities.

The Catalyst for Change

The turning point came during an annual review, where a third-party consultant highlighted the lack of open communication as a critical barrier to the company's growth. The feedback was a wake-up call for XYZ-MNO's leadership, especially for the CEO, Alex, who realized the need for a cultural overhaul, starting with how meetings were conducted.

Implementing a New Meeting Culture

Alex introduced a series of changes designed to foster open and honest communication:

- Setting the Stage: At the start of each meeting, Alex emphasized the importance of transparency and the safe space policy. This policy assured team members that their honest opinions and feedback were not just welcome but necessary for the company's success.

- Active Listening Exercises: Meetings began with exercises to practice active listening, ensuring that participants fully engaged with and considered the viewpoints being shared.

- The 'No Interruption' Rule: A strict rule was enforced where speakers were allowed to finish their thoughts without interruption, signaling respect for each speaker's input.

- Encouraging Diverse Perspectives: Alex made it a point to solicit opinions from quieter team members, ensuring a wider range of perspectives was heard.

The Impact

The effects of these changes were not instantaneous, but over time, XYZ-MNO began to see a significant shift:

- <u>Problem-Solving Efficiency</u>: With open dialogue, the team could quickly get to the heart of issues. The IDS (Identify, Discuss, Solve) process became more effective as team members felt comfortable laying all aspects of a problem on the table.

- <u>Innovation Spike</u>: A culture of honesty led to more creative solutions and ideas being shared, as employees no longer feared ridicule or dismissal. This environment of psychological safety spurred innovation.

- <u>Enhanced Team Cohesion</u>: As team members became accustomed to sharing openly, trust within the team grew. This trust led to stronger collaborations and a sense of camaraderie that had been missing.

- <u>Increased Accountability</u>: Open communication made it easier to address accountability, as team members were more willing to take ownership of their actions and their outcomes, knowing that their honesty would be met with support rather than punishment.

A Real-World Example

A pivotal moment showcasing the success of these changes was during a critical project review meeting. The project was behind schedule, and the traditional approach would have likely involved assigning blame and creating a tense atmosphere. Instead, the team utilized their new communication norms to openly discuss what went wrong, identify gaps in planning and execution, and collaboratively develop a plan to get back on track. This meeting not only resolved the immediate issue but also served as a model for future problem-solving sessions.

Reflecting on the Journey

In conversation, Alex shared reflections on the journey:

- "Creating a Culture Takes Time": Changing the meeting culture didn't happen overnight. It required consistent effort and reinforcement of the importance of open communication.

- "Vulnerability is a Strength": By leading with vulnerability, Alex showed that it was okay to admit mistakes or not have all the answers, which encouraged others to do the same.

- "Feedback is a Gift": Re-framing how feedback was perceived – going from   criticism to a gift meant to foster growth and learning – was key to encouraging honest exchanges.

The Takeaway

XYZ-MNO's story is a testament to the transformative power of encouraging open and honest communication in meetings. By creating a safe environment where all members felt comfortable sharing their thoughts and concerns, XYZ-MNO not only enhanced its problem-solving capabilities and innovation but also fostered a culture of trust and respect. This case study underscores the critical role that communication plays in the success of a team and highlights that, in the fast-paced and often high-stakes world of business, the most powerful tool at our disposal might just be the ability to talk openly and listen sincerely.

#12 Implement a Parking Lot (aka Tangent Bin)

In the bustling heart of Silicon Valley, there's a tale that quite perfectly encapsulates the essence of efficiency and focus in meetings. It's the story of XYZ-MNO, a mid-sized software development company that learned the hard way how crucial it is to keep meetings on track. Their journey towards implementing a "parking lot" system for off-agenda topics is not just a testament to improved productivity but a lesson in maintaining the integrity of meeting objectives.

The Scenario Before

XYZ-MNO was like many tech companies, thriving on innovation and creativity. However, their meetings were a different story. Picture this: A weekly team meeting intended to last an hour would routinely spill over into two, sometimes even three hours. The culprit? Tangential conversations.

Meetings would start with a clear agenda, but as soon as someone mentioned a new idea or a problem not on the agenda, down the rabbit hole they would go. While sometimes fruitful, these detours often left little time for the original agenda, leading to frustration and a sense of unproductiveness among team members.

The Catalyst for Change

The turning point came during a quarterly review when the leadership team noticed a concerning trend: despite the lengthy meetings, key objectives were not being met, and project timelines were slipping. The team realized they needed a structured approach to manage off-topic discussions without stifling creativity. Enter the concept of the "parking lot."

Implementing the Parking Lot

The idea was simple yet revolutionary for XYZ-MNO. Whenever an off-topic issue arose during a meeting, it would be noted in the "parking lot" – a literal whiteboard in the room initially, and later a shared digital document for remote participants. These items would be acknowledged but saved for discussion at a more appropriate time, either in a dedicated meeting or through other channels.

The Impact

Meetings Became More Productive: With the parking lot system in place, meetings became more focused. The team could quickly navigate through the agenda, ensuring all planned topics were thoroughly discussed and actioned upon.

Increased Respect for Time: The visible commitment to stick to the agenda and respect everyone's time fostered a culture of punctuality and preparation. Team members started coming to meetings more prepared, knowing that the window for discussion was finite.

Enhanced Creativity and Problem-Solving: Initially, some team members were concerned that the parking lot system would dampen spontaneity and creative discussions. However, the opposite happened. Knowing that their ideas and concerns would be captured and addressed later allowed everyone to focus more intently on the topic at hand, leading to deeper and more meaningful discussions.

Better Tracking of Issues: The parking lot didn't just help keep meetings on track; it also served as a valuable repository of ideas and issues that might have otherwise been overlooked. Regular review of the parking lot items became a part of the team's workflow, ensuring that nothing fell through the cracks.

A Real-Life Example

Consider the case of a new feature proposal that was brought up during a meeting focused on the upcoming product release. Instead of derailing the meeting's agenda, the idea was placed in the parking lot. The result? The product release planning was completed efficiently, and a separate, dedicated session was later held to explore the new feature, which eventually became one of the product's standout offerings.

The Conversational Shift

In team meetings, the conversation shifted from a free-for-all brainstorming session to more focused discussions. *"Let's park that idea and revisit it later"* became a common phrase, signaling to the team that while their contributions were valued, there was a time and place for every discussion.

Reflections from the Team

Months into using the parking lot system, the team reflected on its impact. Many expressed how it transformed the meeting culture at XYZ-MNO, making discussions more purposeful and time-efficient. There was a collective acknowledgment that the parking lot system was instrumental in this transformation.

Final Thoughts

XYZ-MNO's journey from chaotic, unproductive meetings to structured, efficient gatherings underscores the power of simple organizational tools like the parking lot. By ensuring that off-agenda topics were noted but not forgotten, XYZ-MNO was able to maintain the focus and integrity of their meetings, ultimately leading to a more productive and engaged team.

This story is more than just a case study; it's a blueprint for any team looking to enhance meeting efficiency without quashing the spontaneity and creativity that often spark the most innovative ideas. It proves that with the right systems in place, meetings can be both productive and a breeding ground for future innovation.

#13 Use Technology Wisely

In today's fast-paced work environment, the effective use of technology in meetings is not just a convenience —it's a necessity. Let's take a closer look at how one company, "XYZ-MNO," transformed its approach to meetings by wisely incorporating technology, specifically through the use of project management tools and shared documents. This real case study will illustrate the importance of technology in keeping meetings productive, focused, and aligned with the team's goals.

The Scenario at XYZ-MNO

XYZ-MNO, a startup specializing in renewable energy solutions, was on the brink of significant growth. However, as the team expanded, the founders noticed a decline in meeting productivity. Ideas were discussed, but follow-through was lacking. Action items were agreed upon but quickly forgotten. The team was growing frustrated with the lack of progress on key projects.

The Turning Point

The leadership team realized that the root of the problem was not a lack of ideas or motivation but rather a lack of organization and accountability. Their meetings were traditional: agendas sent out via email, notes taken on individual laptops, and action items tracked (or not tracked) in various personal to-do lists. There was no central system for managing meeting outcomes or tracking progress in real-time.

Implementing Change

Determined to turn things around, XYZ-MNO decided to use technology to overhaul their meeting structure. They introduced a project management tool that would serve as a single source of truth for all projects and tasks discussed in meetings. Additionally, they started using shared documents for meeting agendas and notes, accessible to the entire team in real-time.

How Technology Made a Difference

1. Centralized Information: With the project management tool, every task, no matter how small, was recorded and assigned during the meeting. This centralization of information meant that nothing fell through the cracks.

2. Real-Time Collaboration: Shared documents for agendas and notes changed how meetings were conducted. Team members could add agenda items before the meeting and contribute to the notes during the meeting, fostering a collaborative environment.

3. Visibility and Accountability: The visibility of tasks and their status in the project management tool created a sense of accountability among team members. Everyone knew who was responsible for what and by when.

4. <u>Streamlined Follow-Up</u>: Instead of sifting through email threads, the team could now easily refer to the project management tool to check on the progress of tasks. This made follow-up meetings more focused and productive.

The Impact on Meetings and Beyond

The introduction of these technological tools transformed XYZ-MNO's meetings from aimless discussions to action-oriented sessions. Meetings became shorter, yet more was accomplished. The team felt more engaged, knowing that their contributions were being recorded and would lead to tangible outcomes.

But the benefits extended beyond just meetings:

- <u>Project Efficiency</u>: Projects moved forward more smoothly because tasks were clearly defined and progress was transparent.

- <u>Team Morale</u>: The frustration of forgotten tasks and missed opportunities decreased, leading to improved morale and a stronger sense of team cohesion.

- <u>Innovation</u>: With meetings becoming more efficient, the team had more time to focus on innovation and creative problem-solving.

Conversational Insights from XYZ-MNO

Reflecting on the transformation, the CEO of XYZ-MNO shared, "Integrating technology into our meetings wasn't just about keeping better track of what we discussed. It was about changing our culture to one where accountability and collaboration are at the forefront. It's made a world of difference."

A project manager added, "Seeing my tasks and deadlines in the context of the team's goals has really helped me prioritize my work. Plus, being able to contribute to meeting agendas ahead of time means we're all coming in more prepared and focused."

Conclusion

XYZ-MNO's story is a powerful example of how using technology wisely—through project management tools and shared documents—can revolutionize meetings and, by extension, the way a team works together. It shows that with the right tools and approach, meetings can become a driving force for productivity and innovation, rather than a dreaded time sink.

#14 Seek Feedback For Continuous Improvement

In the bustling world of tech startups, where innovation is the currency and agility the creed, there's a tale that stands out—a story of a team that turned the mundane into a mechanism for growth. This is the journey of XYZ-PQR, a mid-sized app development company, that learned the profound impact of continuous improvement in their meetings, transforming them from time-consuming necessities to pivotal strategy sessions. Let's dive into how they did it, with a focus on soliciting and incorporating feedback to refine their meeting processes.

The Prequel: A Familiar Struggle

XYZ-PQR was no stranger to the rapid pace of the tech industry, but as they grew, so did the complexity of their projects and the number of their team meetings. Initially, these gatherings felt like ticking boxes rather than propelling projects forward. The leadership team sensed the growing frustration but couldn't pinpoint the remedy.

A Spark of Insight

The turning point came during an annual retreat, a rare moment of reflection away from the daily grind. The CEO, Alex, casually asked for feedback on various aspects of the company's operations. What he didn't expect was the avalanche of thoughts about the meetings. "Too long," some said. "Unfocused," others added. But it wasn't just complaints; there were suggestions, ideas for improvement that no one had voiced before.

The Experiment Begins

Encouraged by the candid feedback, Alex proposed an experiment: a three-month period of continuous improvement for meetings. The goal was simple—make meetings more effective and less of a chore. They started with small, manageable changes:

- <u>Surveys after every meeting</u>: Quick, anonymous surveys were sent to gather immediate feedback on meeting effectiveness, participation, and areas for improvement.

- <u>Open forum discussions</u>: Monthly sessions were dedicated to discussing the meeting culture openly, without judgment, allowing everyone to contribute ideas.

- <u>A/B testing meeting formats</u>: They experimented with different meeting lengths, formats, and frequencies to see what worked best for their team dynamics.

The Results: A Transformative Shift

The impact was both immediate and profound. Here's what they found:

- <u>Increased Engagement</u>: As team members saw their suggestions being implemented, their investment in meetings surged. Participation rates soared, and the quality of discussions improved dramatically.

- <u>Enhanced Productivity</u>: By refining their meeting structure based on feedback, XYZ-PQR discovered the sweet spot for meeting length and frequency that maximized productivity without causing burnout.

- <u>Heightened Morale</u>: The process of continuous improvement made team members feel valued and heard, leading to an overall boost in morale and job satisfaction.

Continuous Improvement in Action

One significant change was the introduction of a "focus topic" for each meeting, based on team suggestions. This adjustment ensured that meetings had a clear purpose, and discussions remained on track. Additionally, the feedback highlighted a desire for more recognition of team achievements. As a response, a segment was added to celebrate weekly wins, big or small, fostering a positive meeting atmosphere.

The Ripple Effect

The benefits of this new approach to meetings extended beyond the conference room. Project timelines became more predictable as decisions made during meetings were more focused and actionable. Cross-departmental communication improved as well, as the refined meeting format was adopted company-wide, breaking down silos and enhancing collaboration.

Conversational Reflections

In a candid conversation, a team lead shared, "I used to dread meetings, seeing them as a blockade in my day. Now, they're opportunities—to learn, decide, and *celebrate*. It's a complete 180."

Another team member added, "Seeing my feedback turn into action has been incredibly empowering. It's not just about having better meetings; it's about feeling part of something bigger, shaping how we work together."

Lessons from XYZ-PQR

XYZ-PQR's story is a testament to the power of continuous improvement, especially when applied to the often-overlooked domain of meetings. By regularly soliciting feedback and being genuinely open to change, they turned a pain point into a strategic asset.

The Takeaway

The journey of XYZ-PQR teaches us an invaluable lesson: the path to efficiency and team harmony often lies in listening, adapting, and evolving. Meetings, like any other aspect of work, can always be improved. The key is to keep asking, "How can we do this better?" and to have the courage to implement the answers. Continuous improvement in meetings isn't just about making them shorter or more bearable; it's about creating spaces where ideas flourish, decisions are made with confidence, and every voice is heard and valued.

#15 Celebrate Wins

In the bustling world of startups, where the atmosphere is as dynamic as the market itself, the power of positivity can sometimes be the unsung hero that propels a team forward. Let's dive into the story of ABC-GHI— a small but ambitious tech startup that unlocked the secret to boosting team morale and productivity by simply starting their meetings with a celebration of wins.

The Backstory

ABC-GHI had its fair share of ups and downs. Like many startups, they faced the challenges of tight deadlines, fierce competition, and the constant pressure to innovate. Amidst this high-stress environment, the morale started to wane, and with it, productivity began to dip. Meetings had become somber affairs, primarily focused on what was going wrong, what was behind schedule, and the hurdles that lay ahead.

A Simple Shift

The turning point came during one particularly tough quarter, when Mia, the team leader, noticed the gloom that had settled over her team. Determined to turn things around, she introduced a small, yet significant, change to the meeting structure: every meeting would start with a round of sharing recent successes, no matter how small. This wasn't just about celebrating major milestones; it was about recognizing the daily victories that often went unnoticed.

The Impact

<u>Immediate Uplift in Atmosphere</u>: From the very first meeting, the change was palpable. Sharing successes brought smiles, laughter, and a sense of pride. The team began to look forward to meetings as a space to not only discuss challenges but to celebrate their achievements.

<u>Enhanced Team Cohesion</u>: Celebrating wins created a culture of appreciation and recognition within the team. Members became more supportive of each other, acknowledging their colleagues' efforts and contributions. This fostered a stronger, more cohesive team dynamic.

<u>Boosted Motivation</u>: Hearing about successes, big and small, served as a powerful motivator. It reminded the team of their capabilities and the impact of their work. This renewed sense of purpose propelled them to tackle challenges with increased vigor.

<u>Shift in Perspective</u>: Starting meetings on a positive note helped reframe challenges as opportunities. The team shifted from a problem-centric view to a solution-oriented mindset, approaching obstacles with optimism and creativity.

The Ripple Effect

The benefits of celebrating wins extended beyond just the meetings. It cultivated an environment where positive feedback and encouragement were the norms, not the exception. This had a profound effect on the team's overall morale and productivity.

- <u>Increased Engagement</u>: Team members became more engaged and proactive in their roles. They were not just working to avoid negative outcomes but were driven by the desire to contribute to the team's success.

- <u>Improved Communication</u>: The practice of sharing successes improved communication across the team. It encouraged openness and made it easier for team members to share their ideas and suggestions.

- <u>Resilience in the Face of Setbacks</u>: By focusing on what they had achieved, the team built resilience. Setbacks were no longer demoralizing but seen as temporary hurdles on the path to success.

Conversational Reflections

Mia reflected on the transformation, saying, "It's amazing how a few minutes of positivity can change the entire tone of a meeting and even the course of a day.

Celebrating our wins has reminded us all why we do what we do."

A team member shared, "I used to dread meetings, expecting a rundown of everything that was going wrong. Now, I look forward to hearing about our wins. It's a reminder that we're moving forward, even when it doesn't feel like it."

Conclusion

ABC-GHI' story highlights the transformative power of starting meetings by celebrating wins. This simple practice can uplift the team spirit, enhance motivation, and foster a positive and resilient workplace culture. It's a testament to the fact that in the fast-paced and often daunting world of startups, taking a moment to acknowledge and celebrate each step forward can be the key to sustained success and growth.

#16 Use Visual Aids

In the bustling world of tech startups, where data drives decisions and the pace is relentless, one company, ABC-JKL, discovered the transformative power of visual aids in making their meetings not just bearable but genuinely engaging and productive. This isn't just a story about adding some pretty pictures to a presentation; it's about how ABC-JKL turned their data review sessions from a dreaded chore into the highlight of the team's week. So, grab another coffee, and let's dive into this tale.

The Pre-Visualization Era

ABC-JKL had all the hallmarks of a successful startup: innovative products, a passionate team, and a data-driven approach. However, their weekly data review meetings were a different story. Picture this: a room full of brilliant minds, eyes glazed over, as slide after slide of raw data and bulleted lists were projected on the screen. The meetings were crucial, but the delivery was uninspiring. Critical insights were getting lost in the sea of numbers, and engagement was at an all-time low.

The Aha! Moment

Enter Alex, ABC-JKL's newly appointed Head of Product. Alex, with a background in data visualization, was quick to diagnose the problem. The data wasn't the issue; it was how the data was being presented. Alex proposed an experiment: for the next meeting, instead of the usual slides, they would use charts, graphs, and scorecards to represent the week's key metrics.

The Transformation

The change was nothing short of revolutionary. Here's what happened:

1. <u>Improved Understanding</u>: Complex data sets were simplified into clear, easy-to-understand visuals. Trends that were once buried in spreadsheets became glaringly obvious. Suddenly, everyone in the room could grasp the nuances of the data without a degree in statistics.

2. <u>Increased Engagement</u>: With the data now visually appealing, team members found it easier to stay focused. The visuals sparked curiosity and prompted questions, leading to lively discussions that had been absent in previous meetings.

3. <u>Enhanced Decision-Making</u>: Visual aids helped the team quickly identify areas of success and concern, speeding up the decision-making process. What used to take a lengthy debate was now evident at a glance, thanks to comparative graphs and heat maps.

4. <u>Empowered Team Members</u>: Seeing the data represented visually gave team members the confidence to contribute their insights. The meetings became collaborative workshops rather than one-way presentations. Everyone felt they had a stake in interpreting the data and suggesting action items.

Celebrating the Wins

But Alex didn't stop there. Recognizing the importance of morale, each meeting began with a review of "wins" represented visually. Successes, big and small, were highlighted in vibrant graphs, showing growth trends, milestone achievements, and targets met. This not only set a positive tone for the meetings but also reminded the team of their progress and collective impact, boosting motivation.

The Ripple Effect

The impact of incorporating visual aids into ABC-JKL's meetings reached beyond just making data review more engaging. It fostered a culture of transparency and inclusivity. Team members, regardless of their role or expertise in data analysis, could now actively participate in discussions about the company's direction and strategy.

Lessons Learned

Reflecting on the journey, Alex shared some key takeaways:

- <u>Visuals Speak Louder Than Words</u>: Complex information is more easily digested and remembered when presented visually.

- <u>Engagement Drives Insight</u>: An engaged team is a thinking team. Visual aids draw people in and encourage active participation.

- *Celebrate Every Success*: Starting meetings with visual celebrations of wins sets a positive tone and keeps the team motivated.

Conclusion

ABC-JKL's story is a testament to the power of visual aids in transforming meetings from mundane to meaningful. By making data review sessions more engaging and informative with charts, graphs, and scorecards, they not only enhanced understanding and decision-making but also cultivated a more inclusive and motivated team culture. This case study underscores a universal truth in the business world: the right visual aids can turn data into stories, and stories are what truly captivate and inspire us.

#17 Offer Training and Development

In the bustling world of tech startups, where innovation moves at the speed of light, the story of XYZ-PQR, a small but ambitious app development company, shines a light on the transformative power of integrating training and development into the fabric of meeting participation and leadership. This narrative explores how dedicating resources to educate their team not only improved the quality of their meetings but also propelled the company towards unprecedented growth.

The Backstory of XYZ-PQR

XYZ-PQR started, as many do, with a tight-knit team of passionate innovators eager to disrupt the app development scene. Their early meetings were informal—often just a group of friends brainstorming over coffee. However, as the company grew, so did the complexity of their projects and the size of their team. It became apparent that the casual approach to meetings that worked in their infancy was no longer effective.

Identifying the Gap

Lucas, the CEO, noticed a trend: meetings were becoming increasingly unproductive. Decisions took too long, actions were unclear, and not all voices were heard. After a particularly unfruitful quarterly planning session, he decided it was time for a change. The team had the expertise and the ideas but lacked the skills to conduct and participate in meetings effectively.

The Pivot to Training and Development

Lucas introduced a comprehensive training program focused on effective meeting participation and leadership. The goal was clear: empower every team member, regardless of their position, with the skills to contribute to, lead, and facilitate meetings effectively.

The Training Program

The program covered everything from setting clear agendas, facilitating discussions, active listening, to summarizing action items. It also included leadership training for potential meeting leaders, teaching them how to encourage participation, manage time effectively, and handle conflict.

Immediate Impact

The effect of the training was noticeable from the very first meeting post-training. Discussions were more focused, decisions were reached faster, and there was a notable increase in engagement from all team members.

Long-Term Benefits

But the benefits of the training went beyond just improved meeting efficiency:

- <u>Empowered Team Members</u>: Employees felt more confident in their ability to contribute meaningfully to discussions, leading to a richer pool of ideas and perspectives.

- <u>Enhanced Leadership Skills</u>: Potential leaders identified through the training program brought fresh approaches to meeting management, invigorating the team with new energy.

- <u>Improved Project Outcomes</u>: With more effective meetings, projects progressed more smoothly, with clearer objectives, better-defined roles, and more timely completions.

- <u>Cultural Shift</u>: The training fostered a culture of continuous improvement, encouraging everyone to seek out ways to make meetings even more effective.

A Case Study in Success

Six months after the training was rolled out, XYZ-PQR launched its most ambitious project yet—a groundbreaking app that received industry-wide acclaim. This success was, in no small part, attributed to the improved effectiveness of their team meetings. The ability to come together, efficiently hash out details, assign tasks, and follow through on action items was a game-changer.

Conversational Insights

Reflecting on the journey, Lucas shared, "Investing in our team's ability to meet effectively was one of the best decisions we ever made. It's like we unlocked a whole new level of productivity and innovation."

A team member, Maya, added, "I used to dread meetings, feeling like I never knew when to speak up or how to contribute. The training changed all that. Now, I look forward to meetings as a chance to share my ideas and hear from others."

Wrapping Up

The story of XYZ-PQR is a compelling testament to the power of investing in training and development for effective meeting participation and leadership. By recognizing the potential of their team and providing them with the tools to unlock that potential, XYZ-PQR not only improved the quality of their meetings but also set the stage for a culture of continuous improvement and success.

This case study serves as a reminder that the foundation of any successful organization lies not just in the ideas or the technology it produces but in the effectiveness of its people. Training and development in meeting participation and leadership can be a catalyst for unlocking that effectiveness, driving both individual growth and organizational success.

#18 Address Dominance

In any team or meeting scenario, the balance of conversation is crucial. It's a common pitfall: one or two voices begin to dominate, overshadowing the rest, and suddenly, the collective wisdom of the group is narrowed down to the loudest opinions. Let's look at how "XYZ-DEF," a burgeoning graphic design firm, tackled this challenge head-on, turning their meetings from monologues into dynamic exchanges of ideas.

The Early Days of XYZ-DEF

XYZ-DEF started as a small, tight-knit team where brainstorming sessions felt like coffee chats with friends. However, as the company grew, so did the diversity of its team and the complexity of its projects. Meetings began to change tone; they became less about collaboration and more about endurance, dominated by a few senior team members. Ideas from newer or quieter team members were seldom heard.

The Turning Point

Lucy, a recent hire with a background in organizational psychology, noticed the imbalance. She observed that while the dominant voices often had valuable insights, the quieter team members also had brilliant, albeit unheard, ideas. Lucy proposed a simple yet potentially transformative idea: actively manage meeting dynamics to ensure balanced participation.

Implementing Change

With the support of management, Lucy led a workshop on effective communication for the whole team, emphasizing the importance of diverse input in creative work. She introduced tools and rules designed to redistribute the conversational space:

- "The Talking Stick" Approach: A metaphorical (sometimes literal) object passed around to signify whose turn it was to speak, ensuring everyone had the opportunity to contribute without interruption.

- Time Limits for Contributions: Each person had a set time to share their ideas, ensuring lengthy monologues were curtailed.

- Round Robin Check-ins: Meetings began with a round-robin format, where everyone gave a brief update or shared an idea, ensuring all voices were heard from the start.

- Encouragement of Quiet Voices: Leaders were trained to actively solicit input from those who hadn't spoken much, often with, *"Let's hear from someone who hasn't had a chance to share yet."*

The Outcome

The impact was palpable. Meetings became more dynamic and inclusive. Ideas flowed more freely, and the quality of XYZ-DEF's projects improved significantly due to the richer tapestry of insights.

A Closer Look at the Benefits

1. <u>Enhanced Creativity</u>: With a wider range of perspectives, the team began to push the boundaries of their designs. Projects took on new, innovative directions that hadn't been considered before.

2. <u>Increased Engagement</u>: Team members who previously felt sidelined were now more engaged. They knew their voices mattered, leading to increased morale and a stronger sense of belonging.

3. <u>Improved Decision-Making</u>: Decisions were now informed by a broader set of viewpoints, leading to more well-rounded and effective outcomes.

4. <u>Leadership Development</u>: The process helped identify potential leaders who had previously been overshadowed. Their ability to contribute under the new system showcased their skills and insights.

Conversational Insights

In a candid conversation, a once-dominant team member shared, "I didn't realize how much I was monopolizing the discussions until we started making these changes. It's been a humbling and enlightening experience. I'm learning so much from everyone now."

A previously quiet team member noted, "I used to dread meetings, feeling like there was no point in me being there. Now, I'm excited to share my ideas. It feels like we're truly a team."

Continuous Improvement

XYZ-DEF didn't stop there. They made it a point to regularly review their meeting processes, always looking for ways to enhance inclusivity and collaboration. This commitment to continuous improvement ensured that as the team evolved, so did their approach to meetings.

Final Thoughts

XYZ-DEF's journey from dominated discussions to balanced, inclusive conversations serves as a powerful case study in the importance of addressing dominance in meetings. It highlights that when all voices are heard, the collective potential of a team is truly unleashed. This approach doesn't just improve meetings; it transforms them into engines of innovation and engagement, fostering a culture where everyone feels valued and heard.

#19 Follow-Up

In the bustling world of tech startups, where the pace is relentless and the stakes are high, the effectiveness of team meetings can be the linchpin for success or failure. Let's dive into the story of ABC-MNO—a company that learned the hard way how crucial follow-up is after meetings, and how transforming this aspect of their process became a game-changer for their business.

The Before Scenario

ABC-MNO, a once-small startup that had rapidly grown into a significant player in the renewable energy sector, found itself grappling with a problem. Despite having a talented team and groundbreaking products, progress on key projects was frustratingly slow. The leadership team was baffled. Meetings were productive, ideas were plentiful, and decisions seemed clear—at least, that's what everyone thought as they left the conference room.

The Turning Point

During a particularly reflective annual review, a junior team member, Alex, made a casual observation that struck a chord: "We talk a lot, decide a lot, but I often leave wondering, 'What next?'" This simple question sparked a realization. The company had no systematic way of tracking decisions made during meetings or ensuring that action items were carried out afterward.

Implementing a Follow-Up Process

Determined to tackle this issue head-on, the leadership team, spearheaded by the CEO and Alex, decided to overhaul their follow-up process. Here's what they did:

1. <u>Clear Action Items</u>: They ensured that every meeting ended with clear, concise action items, each assigned to a specific person with a deadline.

2. <u>Communication</u>: Immediately after each meeting, a summary email was sent to all attendees, outlining decisions made, action items assigned, and deadlines.

3. <u>Tracking Progress</u>: They introduced a project management tool that allowed everyone to update the status of their tasks, visible to the entire team.

4. <u>Accountability Checks</u>: Weekly check-ins were scheduled to review the progress of action items, providing an opportunity for team members to ask for help or resources if they were hitting roadblocks.

The Results

The impact of these changes was both immediate and profound. Here's what happened:

- <u>Increased Clarity</u>: The post-meeting summaries and the project management tool ensured that everyone left meetings with a clear understanding of what was expected of them.

- <u>Boosted Productivity</u>: With clear deadlines and visible progress tracking, team members were more motivated to complete their tasks. The project management tool became a source of accountability and a little healthy competition.

- <u>Enhanced Team Dynamics</u>: The weekly accountability checks turned into productive sessions where challenges were discussed openly, and solutions were brainstormed collaboratively. It fostered a sense of team solidarity and support.

- <u>Faster Project Completion</u>: Projects that had been lagging suddenly picked up pace. The new follow-up process ensured that decisions made in meetings translated into action, propelling projects forward.

Conversational Insights

Reflecting on the transformation, the CEO shared, "It was a wake-up call to realize that our meetings were essentially in a vacuum. We'd decide and then disperse, without a clear path from discussion to action. Changing that has been pivotal."

Alex, whose observation sparked the change, noted, "Seeing my casual comment lead to such a fundamental shift has been incredible. It's made me realize the power of speaking up and the importance of follow-through."

Conclusion

ABC-MNO' journey from meeting frustration to streamlined productivity is a powerful testament to the importance of follow-up. By ensuring that decisions and action items from meetings were clearly communicated and followed up on, they not only improved their project completion rates but also enhanced team morale and individual accountability. It's a lesson that any organization, regardless of size or industry, can learn from: the true value of a meeting is realized not just in the moment of agreement, but in the actions that follow.

#20 Establish Clear Action Items

Imagine a dynamic tech startup, let's call it "ABC-PQR," that's on the fast track to innovation but has been hitting some bumps when it comes to team meetings. Despite the groundbreaking ideas flying around, the team often left meetings feeling more confused than when they started. That's until they implemented one game-changing strategy: ensuring that each discussion point results in clear action items with assigned responsibilities and deadlines. Let's dive into this real case study to explore why this approach is so crucial.

The Challenge at ABC-PQR

ABC-PQR was a place buzzing with energy and potential. Their team meetings, however, were a different story. They had all the right ingredients: passionate team members, innovative ideas, and a collaborative spirit. Yet, the follow-through after meetings was lackluster. Projects were moving at a snail's pace, deadlines were missed, and frustration was mounting. The issue? A lack of clear action items and assigned responsibilities post-meeting.

The Turning Point

The leadership team, led by the charismatic yet pragmatic CEO, Alex, decided it was time for a change. Alex introduced a new rule: no discussion would end without defining clear action items, assigning them to specific team members, and setting firm deadlines. This simple shift was about to make a world of difference.

Implementing the Change

The first few meetings under the new rule were a bit awkward. Team members were not used to being so disciplined about wrapping up discussions with action items. However, Alex and the management team were patient, guiding each conversation to a clear conclusion with actionable next steps. They used shared documents to record these actions, making them visible to everyone in real time.

The Impact

1. Increased Accountability: With action items assigned to specific individuals, there was no ambiguity about who was responsible for what. This clarity led to a significant increase in accountability and a decrease in the "I thought someone else was handling it" syndrome.

2. Improved Productivity: The clear delineation of next steps and deadlines meant that team members could hit the ground running post-meeting. There was no longer any confusion about what needed to be done, which led to a noticeable uptick in productivity.

3. Enhanced Team Morale: As the team started seeing real progress and tangible outcomes from their meetings, morale soared. Meetings were no longer seen as time-wasters but as catalysts for action and advancement.

4. <u>Better Tracking of Progress</u>: With each action item documented and deadlines set, tracking the progress of various projects became much easier. This visibility allowed for timely interventions when things were off track.

A Closer Look: A Specific Project

Let's zoom in on one project that exemplified the success of this approach: the launch of ABC-PQR's new app. In the initial brainstorming meeting, the team came up with dozens of feature ideas. Under the old system, these ideas might have floated around indefinitely. But with the new rule in place, each idea was evaluated, and clear action items were assigned for feasibility studies, design mockups, and prototype development, each with a responsible team member and a deadline.

This structured approach allowed ABC-PQR to go from concept to launch in record time, with the app receiving rave reviews for its innovation and usability. The project became a case study in itself on the effectiveness of clear action items and accountability.

Conversational Insights from the Team

Reflecting on the transformation, Alex shared, "It was about turning our conversations into commitments. Every great idea deserves a plan to bring it to life, and that's what we've achieved."

A developer, Jordan, mentioned, "Knowing exactly what I'm responsible for after each meeting has been a game-changer for me. It's empowering and motivates me to deliver on my commitments."

The Bigger Picture

The success of ABC-PQR in implementing clear action items with assigned responsibilities and deadlines is a powerful testament to the importance of this approach in meeting management. It's a strategy that fosters accountability, clarity, and productivity, transforming meetings from aimless discussions into engines of progress.

Conclusion

The story of ABC-PQR is a compelling illustration of how a simple shift in meeting management can lead to profound improvements in team dynamics, project execution, and overall company success. It underscores the power of clear action items to not only drive progress but also to inspire and motivate a team to achieve great things.

FINAL THOUGHTS

The Meeting Is <u>YOUR</u> Talk Show

Like all "shows" yours has:

- A Producer (the Company)
- A Host (You)
- A Cast (Team members and participants)

The Producer of the show is looking for one thing: RATINGS

Ratings amount to things like:

- Did the show devolve into an ongoing litany of complaints and arguments?
- Did one of the Cast members go off on a tangent and not allow the show to move forward?
- Was anything pressing even discussed and will anything even be done about it?
- Will what was discussed bring in more revenue? More profit?
- (and bear in mind, the Producer may even be in the meeting)!

How do you achieve the highest ratings?

As the Host you are looking for one thing: A GOOD PERFORMANCE

Meetings are a serious endeavor. To get the most out of a meeting you need everyone in the meeting to "be present".

Here's how you (and them) can be: Pretend people all over the world are listening to the show in *real time* - you're "live" on-air and you have to make your audience want to keep tuning in!

Your show has to be **positive, upbeat, entertaining, engaging, and educational**!

The BEST way to ensure your success as a leader in a meeting is to keep the cardinal rule in mind, "<u>what if other people were listening</u>".

Your job is to teach each and every Cast member this Bonus Lesson.

The truth is, we're always being listened to (think Alexa), filmed (security cameras / Ring doorbells), and tracked (your iPhone / Android and especially the

Internet). At all times a good rule of thumb is to always remember "someone is seeing or listening", and if they aren't now, they could.

Wouldn't your meetings improve dramatically with this mindset? Of course they would!

But you say, "I feel like I'm in a position where nothing can be positive, upbeat, entertaining, engaging, or educational!" - *but that's your job*.

You're the host and your audience is expecting it! You have all the tools you need (20 concrete examples are above) in order to make the most out of every meeting.

What about the Cast you say?

The Cast Is Simply Wanting You To Respect Their Time and Themselves

On my radio show I had a great cast around me. That's what really made the show special.

When leading a meeting there is a tendency to believe that you, as the leader/host (Facilitator), are the most important person in the meeting - after all, "it's your show".

But you're not the most important factor in having a successful meeting.

The Cast is!

In order to lead a great meeting you have to make them feel like they are the most important person in the room, individually. A part of the show.

CONCLUSION

By using the 20 lessons in this book you should be able to make the Producer happy, the Cast happy, and YOURSELF happy. Because these lessons work.

Your meetings should be everything everyone hoped to get out of having to be "in a meeting".

As a result, your company could grow and become even more successful.

NOTES